EXP●SURE:

The Scattered Thoughts of a Genius

A Published Journal

by Donamechi Davis

- "A SETBACK is the SETUP for a COMEBACK."

Forward

Please don't do as I do; because I'm far from perfect. But instead follow the spiritually inspired stroke of the pen that paints the portrait like a brush, which will carefully guide you on the journey toward your success. I question if I am qualified to write a self-help book. How can I tell you how to overcome your obstacles when I'm standing stagnate trying to over come mine?

The sheriff knocked on my door at 6am, issuing me a letter of foreclosure. I walked back to my room and sat on the edge of my bed in silence, as my mind immediately raced to find a solution. Usually people wait until they've reached their pinnacle of success before writing a self-help book. However I promise you, that well before this book finds you, I will be okay.

It's interesting how people gravitate to those who are financially stable but mentally unbalanced. I apologize that I don't have a flashy Lamborghini nor a Maserati to capture your attention; but if interested, I'm willing to give you my scattered thoughts. I encourage you to never discredit the power of a man's thoughts, because in all actuality it was someone's thought that created the Lamborghini and the Maserati. Please allow me to give you what pain gave me, in hopes that you will learn from the lesson, without experiencing the dreadful sting.

EXPOSURE, OF SELF December 4, 2009

Hold a crown above those around you demanding that they grow into it. "A man who wants to lead the orchestra must first turn his back to the crowd" As a teenager I asked my mother what my Uncle Gaylanes' Make Up was, she responded by saying that, "he's just a man with standards". It wasn't until I became older when I analyzing the word STANDARD.

The dictionary describes it as "principles of conduct informed by notions of honor and decency." I adopted this mindset with the thought that the lifestyle would immediately become pleasant. I was wrong. A standard creates an immediate separation therefore it becomes extremely difficult to associate yourself with those who have different views. Be aware because many will accuse you for acting as though you're better, when in all actuality you just want BETTER. The synonym for standard should be loneness, misinterpreted, persecuted, and separated.

Respect, this is what everyone wants but no one knows the true meaning. Respect is a high regard for someone or something. Do you want to know why no one respects you? The real reason others don't is because you don't first respect yourself.

SELF is important because naturally this is where it all begins. Why is it that you do not have complete concern for self? Instead you put self in harms danger to receive acceptance from others. When you seek more approval from others, than self-approval, you've just given others control of you and your destiny.

Wow **CONTROL**, this is a powerful trait. If you can't first CONTROL self it is impossible to control anyone or anything around you. Self Control reflects self-discipline and through self-discipline you will achieve goals beyond your imagination. Understand that your body (The Child), which is motivated by feelings, is only used to carry out the duties of your coherent mind (The Parent).

Therefore if you allow the body (The Child) to control the mind (The Parent), it is relevant that you shall predict a promised failure. Know your strengths and make a plan to capitalize on them, but just as well, know your weaknesses and transform them into strengths. However this will take SELF CONTROL and DISCIPLINE, to embrace this is **WISDOM**.

NEVER fight **WISDOM** because it is like kicking against a brick wall. Learn to LISTEN and when you begin to LISTEN, everything you wanted to know you will soon learn. DENIAL is a Secret Killer and it will stagnate you from completing your mission. When you are in denial you automatically expose yourself to HARM, disappointment and downfall. Denial is an embezzler of time, energy and growth; this is a MISTAKE that's often made!

In life you are not exempt from making MISTAKES but don't make too many of them. Learn how to become observant; it's more convenient to learn from other people's mistakes than making too many of your own. It does not matter whose mouth the truth comes out of, just take heed. It is foolish to waste energy trying to make wrong right, for this is a BATTLE you will never win. Mistakes are permissible but DON'T ever have so much PRIDE where you MAKE the ultimate MISTAKE of not learning from your MISTAKES.

PRIDE is a false evaluation of SELF. Stop fooling yourself to think you're better than others. The more you are humble the MORE man will exalt you. Live with your back against the wall and you will see everything. Treat people right and you will have more associates than enemies. If you keep your RICHES (Money) a secret, it will be easier to identify your friends from the fakes.

The **greatest INVESTMENT** is education (knowledge); please don't make the mistake of running from education. Education is a very important part of your foundation, it will sustain you. An uneducated man is Limited and it's a very good chance that he will be left behind.

WHY balance? **BALANCE** is important. Never be so high where you cannot touch the BOTTOM and never be so LOW where you cannot reach the top, for this is the art of balance.

WHY ME? LOL (*laugh out loud*) this is a commonly asked question. Fredrick Douglas said, "Without struggle, there is no progress". STOP wasting time feeling sorry for you, blaming others and complaining. Spend more time being grateful for life and focus on how to play the hand you've been given. Your struggles will make you strong and your hard work will make you known.

Exposure, Make the Connection! December 8, 2009
Life is simpler than what you think. It's not always what you know but sometimes it's WHOM you know. My mother use to tell me "Don whatever you want to be in life, **put yourself in that environment."** This advice is key! If you want to be a Millionaire you should first ask yourself "how many associates or friends do I have that are Millionaires?" If the answer is none, there is a problem. You might pose a question, "how do I put myself in a powerful environment."
LISTEN to the Media (radio, Television, News paper) and friends. Be aware of the functions which powerful people will be attending and make sure you are there. The more you're seen in a good lighting and heard at the right time, the better. People adapt to what they're familiar with. Before you attend these events VALUE the importance of

PERCEPTION and Self-CONFIDENCE.
Weak minded people believe everything they see, a majority of what they hear and a fraction of what they feel. Therefore this is why you should use perception as a brush to paint any picture that you desire.
CAMOUFLAGE:

5

Net Work: introduce yourself, hold good conversation, make sure you leave a positive lasting impression and get the contact information.

Follow up: Send an email or text message two or three days later reminding him/her who you are and where you both met. Make sure the message is on a light note, warm up to the person a little before asking them for something.

Make the connection: Put your main focus on hold for a moment. It is important that you value the time of getting to know him/her and allowing them to get to know you. Character, charm, integrity and personality will make you a likeable person. People will open door for you just because they like you. DON'T involve sexual encounters during this process it will only tarnish the process.

As you continue to read about my personal struggles **PLEASE TAKE NOTES**.

EXP⊙

SURE:

- "Do not allow the weakness of your past to hinder the strength of your future"

Rejection and REASON to doubt/Random Reflection

On Thursday September 20, 2012; I met with the Vice President of Warner Brothers writing Program. The mood was great, as our unique personalities quickly connected. A 15-minute meeting soon turned into an hour and a half meeting, as our laughter filled the room and echoed down the hallways. This meeting was important, because it would set the foundation for a strong friendship, which would probably land me a writing gig.

I watched as the VP eagerly leaned forward with a bright smile and inquisitively asked; "so what department are you interested in working for"? A wise man once told me "what's rooted in a man's heart will soon come from his mouth". I inadvertently said, "I want to buy out Time Warner (*Warner Bros Parent Company*). The Vice President thought I was playing, and quickly asked why. I replied by telling him that if I bought out Time Warner then I would surly own Warner Brothers.

I watched as his smile slowly faded to a stern and confused face. The room became silent and cold as I immediately felt like a stranger. He looked at me with the eyes of a parent staring at a foolish child and asked, "May I give you some advice off the books"?

I quickly responded by saying "sure". He made sure to properly package his words while saying " don't continue to talk like that, if you want people at this company to take you serious". I would rather have heard him say, "Young man anything is possible!".

However his response didn't bother me. The fact that he graduated from Howard University (HBCU) and in addition knowing that I was Morehouse Alum didn't bother me. Now that I think about it I wasn't even numb at the fact that he was an African American like myself. Now that I think about it, Mr. Cooper unknowingly prepared me for this moment in 2009.

Mr. Cooper (its who you know) worked in Admissions at Harvard University. Out of 10,000 applicants, only 900 are selected a year. Three days prior before taking my GMAT to enter Harvard University my Uncle Willie Burchette died. Waking up to ear piercing screams from my mother was emotionally devastating. I had no idea that the last time I hugged and kissed my uncle goodbye; would be the last time I would ever hug and kiss my uncle goodbye.

We have no idea how situations affect us because while taking the GMAT I could only think about our last moments together. My application fee for Harvard was $250. I wasn't pleased with my GMAT score but because of the deadline I needed to send the information to the school immediately. I spoke with Mr. Cooper several times, giving me great pointers during the application process. He assured me that he would be looking out for my application.

Weeks later I received a denial letter via email. Full of disappoint I called and asked him why? He responded by saying that my GMAT score was so low that he thought it was a typo, but he didn't stop there. He continued by informing me that I was an embarrassment to Morehouse and until I raise my GPA from a 2.9 to at least a 3.8 he would not recommend that I apply to Harvard again. I was hurt but my emotions didn't stop me from translating the message.

I agree that his approach could have been better. But he was only three years older than me, I'm sure I have not always packaged my words appropriately at the tender age of 27. The fact that he was black nor being a Morehouse Alum didn't bother me. I was too focused to allow his cruel word to slow me down. In addition my Morehouse academic adviser, Ms. Depaul and Ms. Jackson unknowingly prepared me for this moment in 2004.

After my aunt Angela took me to visit the campus, and after being denied five times, Morehouse mistakenly sent me an acceptance letter. But getting in was only half the battle. In late August of 2004 I spoke over the phone with my financial aid advisor as an incoming freshmen at Morehouse College.

He advised me to **NOT** set foot on Morehouse campus without at least $15,000 (Tuition, out of state fees, books, room and board and more) for the first semester. It was Friday and I was supposed to be in Atlanta Georgia on Monday.

Sunday after church I asked my mother if my father found the money, her only response was that "he's working on it." I told my mother that this is a miracle that I would have to see for myself. Sunday night I began packing. My father called me into his dark room as he sat on the edge of the bed in deep thought trying to contemplate ways that he would break the news to me. "Yes dad?"

He looked up at me with a strong face but I knew his heart was heavy. He replied by saying,
 "I really tried, but I couldn't get the money." He was disappointed with himself beyond belief. The lack of funds wasn't the problem; it was the reason behind that lack of fund that convicted his soul. Years of playing, alcoholism, and fast women destroyed him financially. Now that he was in his conscience mind he wanted to give me everything but he had nothing to give.

My heart was full of pain, but it wasn't for me, it was for him. I knew he experienced great guilt beyond my imagination. I watched him as he slowly reached in his pants pocked for his wallet. He pulled out his debit card and said, "it's only $400 dollars on there, I know it's not much, but it's all I have." I took it and said thank you, too focused to allow fear to slow me down. I went to the corner ATM and took out $300 leaving him $100 in his bank and returned his card to him. I walked back into my room, sat on the edge of my bed and continued folding and packing. Tears began to quickly fall from my face. Unknown grounds are the hardest to travel because you don't have the control of knowing the out come.

Where I am concerned Morehouse wasn't just a school. The institution symbolized greatness, intelligence, leadership and more. For over ten years of my academic career I was laughed at and tease by my peers because of my learning disability. I would finally have the chance to transform into someone better than the person I use to be. I woke up early the next morning to a wet pillow full of tears. Grabbed my bags and headed to the Airport. I was determined that Fear (false evidence appearing real) would NOT cloud my vision.

My mind raced whiles sitting on the airplane because I didn't have a clue on where I would stay or how I would get around. Class started Thursday therefore I utilized the next three days in hopes to find scholarship money from the school. I asked God to guide me on what to wear, where to go, whom to talk to, how to talk to them, and what I should talk about. I sat in my academic advisors office and after telling him that I didn't have the money he quickly responded by asking "then why are you hear?" I humbly told him "because I want to go to school." He spoke as though he didn't understand the faith concept that my mother had taught me from a child growing up. He rudely dismissed me from his office and told me that there was nothing that he could do for me.

But before I exited, he told me to go see a lady by the name of Ms. DePaul. A few minutes later I sat in Ms. DePaul's office explaining my situation in depths. She looked up at me with the most confused face I have ever seen even until this day.

She asked me for my mother's number and then told me to stand out in the hall while she spoke to her. The kindest and the most respectful words that she used during the duration of that conversation was "hello, is this Mrs. Davis?" An hour after chewing my mother out she opened her office door and told me to come in and sit down. Inside I was upset that she had the nerve of speaking to my mother in such a manner. But my mother and I both knew that this wasn't the time for getting hung up with EGO.

She told me that there was nothing that she could do for me. My heart dropped as I slowly stood up and told her thank you, but before I exited she told me to go see Ms. Jackson. I did as I was told, and God Knows I will never forget Ms. Jacksons; her words were sharper than a hot knife slicing through butter. She was upset, but then again she had every right to be.

She was mad at my mother because college was something that her and my father should have been saving for since my birth. She was disappointed with my parents for not having the credit score to apply for a loan, and In addition Ms. Jackson was upset with me because I didn't have the proper GPA to make myself eligible for scholarships. Ms. Jackson was so upset she spent almost two hours reading me my rights.

Out of frustration she asked, "if you didn't have the money why did you come?" At the naive age of 18 I sat there in silence, and soon responded by saying, "Because I want to go to school." Afterwards she apologized for her poor choice of words.

However her words didn't bother me because majority of them were true. The fact that she didn't recognize the many sacrifices that my parents DID make, which allowed me to knock on the door of Morehouse didn't bother me either. For the next three days of enrollment I arrived to campus early and left late. I knocked on every door on campus asking for money and I continued to here apologies.

I found myself returning to Ms. Jackson office on the last day of enrollment, asking for money to attend school. She reminded me that there wasn't any money and my GPA was to low to receive and scholarships however she promised me that she would keep me in mind incase anything became available. She directed me to Fredrick Douglas Hall (Morehouse resource center), before entering I read Fredrick Douglas quote that was plaster on the wall "without struggle there is no progress".

The resource center was crowded with students who were last minute enrollers. The day quickly came to an end and there was only thirty-five minutes left before the campus closed for the day. My cousin TJ called me with the exciting news of her successful enrollment. She knew I was happy for her but she sensed that something was wrong. I told her that I was yet to enroll. She ensured me that I could attend her school in Florida and that she had some connections that would allow me to make a smooth transition. I was thankful for her kind gesture but Morehouse was the only school for me.

Within seconds a gentleman in his late thirties, early forties by the name of Tony Rocker approached me asking if my name was Don Davis. I said yes and he advised me to follow him. When arriving to his office he asked if I enjoyed doing community service. I responded by saying "no, but I will do it if it helps me get into school". He looked at me with a straight face and advised me to never say that again.

He placed a thick packet in front of me and told me to sign each page. I had no idea what I was signing but I knew he would soon tell me. As I signed he told me that Ms. Jackson told him all about me, and informed me that the scholarship that he was granting me was filled within the first thirty minutes it opened which was almost a year prior. As I signed, I asked him what happened that a position became available.

He told me that someone mysteriously decided to go to another college last minute, which conveniently left a slot open. Full of question I asked how he knew I was the person Ms. Jackson told him about. He told me that Ms. Jackson told him that I was wearing a suit, and just so happened I was the only student wearing a suit on campus that day. Just when I thought that was amazing he asking me if I knew what I was signing.

I responded by saying "no". He told me that the Bonner Scholarship allowed students the opportunity to provide service for their community. I continued to sign as he momentarily sat in silence.

Then he continued by saying, in return the scholarship would pay for my four years of room and board, cafeteria meals, books, and four years of tuition. My eyes looked up in disbelief as he continued by saying, "and we will give you an additional $525.00 a month for attending Morehouse.

I sat back in my chair as my eyes began to water and I exhaled feeling an emotion of utopia like never before. Mr. Rocker told me that the fight was worth it, and curiously asked me if Ms. Jackson was tuff on me. I told him that I experienced worst, and then I told him about my high school counselor (Mr. Townsend) and My Principle (Von) who unknowingly prepared me for such a moment in 2003.

In 2003 my Aunt (Angela Williams) and I sat in my principle (Von) office. He asked how he could be to our assistance. I expressed my interest in Morehouse College and informed him that part of the application process is that I would need a letter of recommendation. He quickly opened and skimmed my files while I continued to talk. I ensured him that I would work hard to graduate high school with a strong finish. After reading my files he asked me if there were any other colleges that caught my interest.

I told him no, Morehouse was the only college that I would apply to. He smirked and chuckled while asking "what if you get denied, what s your plan B?" I smile and chuckled while saying "I won't get denied."

He thought that reminding me of what I already knew would change my answer. He told me that Morehouse requires a 3.5 GPA before even considering an application. He reminded me that I had a 1.8 GPA, I scored an eleven on my ACT, I read on an 7th grade level, I had been a special ed student since the second grade and if I did get accepted the curriculum is so intense that I probably wouldn't be able to finish my first semester. My auntie (Angela Williams) noticed that my principle was discouraging me and audaciously asked, " will you write the letter?" His response was "NO."

My auntie thanked him for his time as we stood to leave. Before we left he advised me to speck with one of my counselors (Mr. Townsend) because he's a graduate of Morehouse. After listening to him remind me of my shortcomings, I felt myself feeling dumb once again. While walking down the hallway my auntie encouraged me by telling me that I was smart, and that I would make it to Morehouse if I stayed focused and kept the faith.

A week later I took my principles advice and spoke with Mr. Townsend. Mr. Townsend told me that I wasn't ready for a Black Ivy League College; in addition he stated that Morehouse was only for a selected few, and by the looks of my academic and behavioral records, I wasn't one of them. I stared at him in disgust; however I wasn't surprised. I wasn't bothered that Mr. Townsend and Von was both African Americans, Nor was I upset that neither of them felt the personal responsibility of mentoring me. I was only seventeen. But it wasn't the first time someone made me feel inadequate, I've been rejected taunted and teased majority of my academic life. These people had reason to doubt me because I first doubted myself. But I knew, one day, if I kept the focus and kept the faith in GOD (its who you know), it would all change.

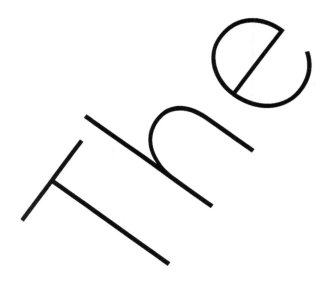

Scattered

Sacrifice 2010 Random Reflection

The grotesque smell of alcohol and drug addicted men; was strong enough to make me vomit twice. As I was forced to hold my bowls because the restroom floor was caked up with old urine that flies immediately flocked to. The strong stench was unbearable, but that was my least concern. I laid in a one sheeted bed. I positioned my body in a fetal position, with my bag clenched to my chest, and my shoelaces tied tight and knotted.

I barely blinked as my eyes pierced through the darkness, alert and aware of any danger that could have come my way. I slept in my car for several months therefore I needed one night of rest where I could stretch my legs; however I immediately found out that this wouldn't be that night.

Life is interesting; I attended Harvard University during the day and slept in a shelter or in the backseat of my car at night. I ate once a day because money was thin. I refused to be a financial burden on my parents therefore I did everything I could to make my food stretch.

Once I brought two boxes of dry generic oak meal ($4.98) and ate it for breakfast, lunch and dinner for over a week. If I didn't have the luxury of water, I ate it dry.

Some time I have to shake my head and laugh because I always allowed my pride and ego to get the best of me. I remember visiting the Star Bucks on Harvard Yard (1380 Mass Ave Harvard Yard Cambridge MA) every morning. Instead of buying their oak meal ($5.00 a bowl) I would smuggle in my own and ask for hot water and a bowl. It wasn't long before they caught on. The gentleman that served me kindly told me that his supervisor informed him that he could no longer provide me with hot water however I could order their oatmeal instead. We locked eyes for a few seconds; it was long enough for him to see my pain that I tried to conceal.

Moments after he said "however I'm going to fill up this bowl with hot water, set it on the table but I'm not responsible for what happens to it once I turn my back" I smiled and said thank you. However it was hard for me to stomach the oatmeal because I foolishly felt as though he looked down on me as though I wasn't an equal but instead a charity case. After eating I thanked him again while tipping him my last $10.00. It was dumb but it was worth it, because my pride didn't allow any man the luxury of knowing my struggle, shortcomings or insecurities. When sleeping in my car I would use the restroom late nights at local 24hour CVS or Walgreens. I would always find a police station or a top-notch hotel to park in front of before resting at night.

No one knew my situation because I didn't want to be looked at as anything less than an equal. I showered and changed clothes daily at a community fitness center. I stayed in the library as long as I could and once it closed; I finish my assignments in the back seat of my car. Gas (Car heater) was expensive so I spent many nights shaking and shivering, holding myself trying to stay warm. My eating habits became worst and my immunes system suffered. Days later I laid in the back of my car sick, stuffy, and lightheaded. I couldn't do anything but pray. We take health for granted until it fails us.

My friends and family just saw the acceptance letter from Harvard but they never noticed the struggle that came with it. The prices we pay to live the lives we want to live. My only advise to you is count up the cost and be sure that the struggle is worth the price. Being a leader is a lonely journey, people will be present to help and guide you however you're responsible for your journey. It's hard to give up something you love in HOPE to get something better.

The average person would settle for less, in fear that they will lose the little that they have. The day I realized that nothing is real but GOD, and that everything on earth is a figment of my imagination, was the day I wanted everything that God wanted me to have. Living in fear is living in doubt, and doubt will paralyze possibility.

My brother Warren J Davis Jr. gave me some of the best advise in life. He told me to educate myself, and live a life where no man can ever dictate my future.

I was barely 24 and published my first book (I Am Loyal) when I met Darryl Cooke (Author & international Motivational speaker). The facts neither that I was an author nor that I was a Morehouse grad impressed him. He told me that I was a big fish in a small pond and if I were to make my mark, I would first have to stand and **be recognized amongst giants.**

He stared at me and said, **"I thought you wanted to make movies?"** I responded by saying, "I do." He smirked and said "then why are you still in Chicago?" I had no idea the struggles, the disappointment, the tears, nor the heartaches, which were coming my way.

All I knew is that I had to sacrifice my comfort zone, in hopes to finds something better.

California was my first stop before grad school in Boston. Tears flowed from my eyes, not because I knew that I would be homeless once I stepped off the airplane, but instead it was because I was transitioning from a boy to a man. Being a momma's boy, and knowing that I would never live with my mom and dad again, hurts. **If you pay attention, and take notes you will realize, and appreciate the many lessons that our creator teaches us on this journey called life.**

The sad part is that were so self centered, that all we think about is us, never taking the time to realize that he's building a stronger bond during the struggle. We're so backward that we spend majority of our life paying awful prices for something counterfeit when the real thing is free. We're obsessed with our own agenda refusing to pay attention to the one that he has already written for us. There are many sacrifices that I had to make. Stop fooling yourself! Remove those who you selected in your life and replace them with who God selected for you. This will make the journey to success a lot easier.

Fulfill the real agenda, and the real agenda will fulfill you/Random Reflection

Many want to be great, but only few know where to begin. There are three important components that each individual should discover on the journey of success (Purpose, Passion, and Career (9-5)). Discovering all three is very difficult but how to connect them is the real challenge. It sounds easy but the problem occurs when the career and passion conflicts with your purpose. Your purpose is the God given assignment while on earth. Your passion brings you personal pleasure. Your career finances your lifestyle, allowing you to be your own person.

The conflict will be solved the moment you acknowledge, accept, and pursue your purpose. If you pursue your passion and negate your purpose the transition will be dreadfully difficult, and the void of not fulfilling your purpose will leave you feeling incomplete. Your purpose will be your protection. Your purpose in life is to be a witness, introducing people to God, in hopes that their souls will be saved. The avenue that you chose to travel is something you will have to seek God about. You should always pursue purpose first because the strong spiritual connection will allow God to guide you. One of the worst feelings is the feeling of being lost. When one has no direction, progress becomes stagnate.

Growing up in a spiritual household I always knew that my purpose was to direct people to follow God. During my late teens I told my mother that I didn't know what I wanted to do with my life. She asked me what I was passionate about. I told her that I didn't know. My mother then asked what I enjoyed doing so much, that I would do it for free. I told her that I enjoyed writing. She responded by saying that writing was my passion; and my next step would be to find a career that would support my passion, until the passion can fiscally support itself. Finding a career that I was interested in was difficult until I enrolled into school.

If you choose my rout, I advise you to apply to an elite university, which will give you a known brand for your resume. In addition, it gives you the opportunity to build strong relationships with other great minds of the future. When entering school, be sure to take the core curriculums because it will give you a better idea of what you enjoy. You can never go wrong with majoring in business or technology (the way of the future). Save your refund checks as "show money", when applying for future credit lines, and learn the importance of your credit before it's destroyed.

Have a plan, stay focused, think positive, be proactive, and remember that everything is easier said, than done. As I mentioned in the prior chapters THE MIND IS very POWERFUL, AND WE ALL ARE CONNECTED.

Be sure to create a promising future by utilizing the components of Prayer (talking to God), Meditation (Listening to God), and Visioning (Mental Placement). How can you call God your best friend and you never spend quality time talking with him. I noticed that many of us talk but no one wants to shut up, sit still, and listen. Find a quiet place, close your eyes, and inhale through your nose while mentally repeating, "Let God" and exhaling "and let go". Find your center by mentally escaping and allow God to lead you.

Last but not least, envisioning where you want to be, will place you where you want to be. Thinking is momentary and it doesn't take much effort. However envisioning takes focus and concentration. Close your eyes and visualize your daily operation in the opportunity of your choice (New Job, Driving new Car, Acting in a major Movie). These are just a few techniques to conquering your future.

If you're a creative entrepreneur like myself; utilize college as an opportunity for a summer intern position at a top company, which will soon be your competition. Build strong relationships, which will lead to a secure position upon graduation. Remember that whom you know will get you the job, and what you know will sustain you in the position.

While working, analyze the company and make sure that your business, capitalizes off of their weakness.

Many creative entrepreneurs don't understand the importance of allowing your career to finance your company (entrepreneurial venture). Instead, they feel as though they should put all their energy and efforts into their company in hopes that someone will discover them and support. In all actuality IF YOU DON'T HAVE MONEY OR A STRONG CREDIT LINE YOU CANT DO NOTHING BUT BEG AND STRUGGLE.

As I've gotten older my passion expanded from writing novels to writing movie scripts. I quickly felt a strong conviction as religious leaders told me that the Hollywood entertainment business was of the devil. I understood my purpose, and God approved of the avenue of creating positive film as one of the tools to persuade potential followers. Pastor Donnie was a spiritual leader who supported my vision. While working faithfully under Pastor Donnie Briggs he randomly asked about the career path that I was pursuing. I told him that I have been applying to Warner Bros for over a year; however I have yet to hear anything. He smiled; made a phone call to an acquaintance that was a manager at Warner Bros, and one week later I was hired.

God has an interesting way of reminding us that if we take care of his business he will take care of ours. Many people don't reach their goals for a number of different reasons. You defeat yourself when you become more reactive than proactive. STOP BEING LAZY! Procrastination and disappointment are soul mates; therefore you should not entertain either of the two.

- I need the impossible; therefore I've convinced myself that the impossible is possible!

I Need The Impossible/Random Reflection

"I need the impossible; therefore I have convinced myself that the impossible is possible." By Donamechi Davis

I=(Referring to the quote above) is a reflection of self.

Self= is a reflection of your actions.

Action= is a reflection of your mind

Need= Maslow's hierarchy of needs theory, is made up of five levels.

The first need on the physiological pyramid is BREAHTING/AIR

The most valued possession you have is your heath; understand THAT YOUR NEED IS YOUR PRIORITY...

The problem that you're having in life is that you NEED WHAT YOU WANT AND DON'T WANT WHAT YOU NEED.

Need triggers urgency.

The impossible: Is the giant that separates you from your goal through the emotion of fear.

What is Fear? FALSE EVIDENCE APPEARING REAL!

If you want something, go where it is.

The longer you're around something the less impressive it is and the easier it is to obtain.

Therefore: is the recognition that it takes a sacrifice to get what you want. The problem you're having is that you don't want to sacrifice anything.

I have convinced: Why does the Bible say that a double minded man is unstable in all of his ways?

Have you ever been convinced of something before? If you have you don't second-guess self or the possibility of the vision coming to fruition.

Myself: Stop-wasting time trying to convince everyone else. Stop wasting time looking for others to validate you. Your mindset needs to be as followed; "I don't need you to believe in my dream, I believe in it."

That the impossible is POSSIBLE: Your belief is your fuel to your actions.
How strong you believe in something determines how far you will go to reach your goal.

Your attitude determines your altitude. During your journey to greatness be sure to remember the true definition of the following words.

No: Means not this door, try the other one.

Impossible: Means Possible.

Stop: Means keep going!

• My occupation is being the best me, and never giving up!

Growth

Growth comes when you strive for greatness because good is not good enough.

It's when you become more concerned with quality than quantity.

Growth is building for strength and not for muscle.

Being great is negating your site to embrace your vision.

Its understanding that maturity is the willingness to give up immediate pleasure for long term gain.

You'll grow when you stop evaluating others and began evaluating self.
Growth comes when you seek for Gods purpose for you, disregarding self-purpose.

Growth is putting your wants on hold to supply someone else's needs.

Growth is giving.

Growth comes when you stop complaining about what you don't have and begin being thankful for what you do have.

One will grow when he/she becomes more concerned with wisdom than wealth.

However to embrace this is to understand that true wealth is not financial but instead it's true wisdom. Growth is finding peace during turmoil and embracing the lesson taught from every bad situation.

Growth is listening, reevaluating and applying the plan

Growth is living your life to the fullest therefore when your youth has gone, you will never say "I would've, I should've, I could've."

Growth is setting a standard for self and coming to the conclusion that if you don't value self, self will never be valued.

WHY?

Why am I attracted to broken women who hide their hearts behind deceit? Why am I more attracted to the one who plays with my heart than the one who has my best Interest at heart? Why do I work so hard, for what I think I want, when what I need is right before me? Why do I lie to myself now, when I know that the truth will haunt me forever? Am I mentally sick to inflict long-term hurt on self?

Denying the fact that the one whom I pursue is more poisonous than a rattlesnake. Am I addicted to the game, the person, or the rush of concurring something that can't be tamed? It's interesting how we end up becoming what we chase. Before you know it the fear of being made a fool, stops you from trusting. Why did I hand my happiness over to her in hopes that she would give me joy? Better yet why did I continue to make trades with my heart when I knew it wasn't a fair exchange?

After years of my emotional torment I soon become her, and someone else becomes the victim. I've been blinded by the years of Hurt, now looking for the worst in my mate and never appreciating the good. Once you've been hurt so long you become numb, not wanting to feel the sting so therefore you shut down.

Running away becomes the answer because confronting the situation penetrates feeling and emotion. Now I can't find a good mate because I keep attracting women who are a reflection of self, and I cant trust them because I can't trust myself.

It gets worst because you know karma is real and the games that's been played has mentally disturbed your prior opponents for the rest of their lives. What was it about her, which made me put self in such a position of pain? How did I become so weak that I allowed emotion to overthrow my logic?

Why did I deny self-love for her counterfeit love? If you think that's sick, then the fact that I miss her is twisted and in addition, the fact that I want to return to her like a dog returning to it's own vomit is worst. When she left she left with a part of me, because I have given so much of myself to her.

My mind thirst for a real relationship however I have drifted off so far, I forgot what a real one looks like.

- Don't make assumptions about peoples actions, ASK!

Relationships

"I don't won't anyone who doesn't want me", Trust that this mindset will save you many years of heartaches and tears. Be careful when choosing the mate that you will invest in. The more you invest in a person the more attached you will become. Relationships are not as difficult as you make them.

The problem comes when you invest your precious time, energy and effort, trying to prove your value to someone who is not mature enough to appreciate it. You waste so much precious time analyzing the dysfunctional mind of your mate. However in all actuality you should be spending that time analyzing self because the people you date and surround yourself with is a reflection of who you are. Truth hurts before it sets you free.

Stop convincing yourself that the person you're with is different from what he/she is showing you. It's imperative that you hold to your high standards. I was watching the discovery channel and found that Eagles set higher standards for their mates than most humans do. I was shocked to find out that the female eagle is aware that she can hold her breath longer than a male eagle. Once a female knows that a male eagle is pursuing her, she immediately increases her altitude.

Reaching maximum heights will gradually stop the male eagles breathing ability. However when exceeding maximum heights lungs will surly collapse and the male eagle will surly die. Even though the male is at a disadvantage, if the male eagle shoots down before the female, he has just proven that he is not strong enough to take care of her for the rest of her life.

But if she shoots down before he does he had just proven the opposite, as they both wrap up in each other's wings while spiraling down and they will mate for life.

When you lower your standards, you'll lower your respect, and when you lower your respect you'll soon lower your self-esteem. Dating can be dangerous if you don't utilize it properly. Be careful not to become more emotional than logical. Be careful of who you connect yourself with because their problems will become your problems.

My mother told me that anything that you don't like about your mate will surely be amplified x10 when you're married. Don't attack the action of your mate but instead question the reason behind their action. Prolong sex because it's a gateway to a persons soul which is the emotions of ones spirit.

The prettiest person can be the biggest monster. Sex too soon can mistakenly lead to a seed, which will unhappily connect you both for a lifetime.

It's interesting that everyone wants to discredit the importance of time. When in all actuality time produces experiences that will reveal a persons true character. My mother informed me years ago that it's ok to fool the world but never fool yourself.

You tend to fool yourself because you don't love yourself to the extent that you should, you don't love self because you don't know self and you will never know self until you seek God. God is the only one who can teach you your true value.

When you have a clear understanding of WHO you are you will accept the realization that only God can pair you with who you are built for; during this journey called life. Your partner's genetics goes back further than what stands before you.

Therefore it is imperative that you are aware of his/her generational demonic struggles, because they may be implemented in your future child. No one can fill your void but God, if you rely on your partner to do so you will continually be disappointed.

I'VE LEARNED TO STOP RUSHING THINGS THAT NEED TIME TO GROW.

Thoughts

Hurt

In 2008 I sat in my dorm room with the phone pressed against my ear waiting for my mother to answer. I could tell by her voice that I woke her from her sleep. We always laughed and joked over the phone but this conversation wouldn't be pleasant. I hesitantly asked her, "mama, when was the last time you saw me?" She light heartedly said, "boy you were just here in Chicago two months ago." She noticed my silence, and soon adapted to my solemn mood.

"No mother, when was the last time you saw my face." Not knowing what to expect I sat there hoping for the best. A few seconds went by and she said, "Wow Don, I think you were about six years old." My heart dropped, as chills traveled throughout my body. A fear that I never knew existed, now stared me in the face. Those words revealed a reality that I spent majority of my life denying.

The fact that my best friend didn't know what I looked like crushed me. I immediately wanted my mother to visually see the man that I have become. I wanted her to see how my facial features had drastically changed, and that I wasn't that little boy anymore. In an odd twisted way I felt a dreadful disconnection because she had no idea of what I looked like.

I tried to keep my composure but the disturbing information triggered the emotions that produced my uncontrollable tears. She told me that it was ok, but it wasn't. I wanted my best friend to see the man that she had groomed me to be. I mistakenly associated what she saw, with knowing who I was.

My desire in life has always been to make my mother proud. I knew that we shared every moment emotionally, but I never realized that we didn't share them visually. She saw the picture of our journey much different than I did. I automatically felt like God cheated her, I was upset that he allowed my mother to sit in darkness for over fifteen years. My crying continued as I processed this information.

My mother continued to tell me that it's okay. But it wasn't, I was in the mist of preparing for one of the biggest days of our life (College Graduation), and even though my mom would be there, she wouldn't be able to visually see her son walk across the stage. It was my mother who encouraged me, fought for me and stuck by my side. She believed in, made sacrifices, and reminded me the important of staying focused. In all actuality this wasn't my graduation it was hers.

But now as I sit here years later, at the age of 27, I think of the many lessons that I've learned from her disability. She taught me to stay strong and to never allow someone to count me out because I'm different.

I think back on the years that she struggled to teach me until she couldn't teach me anymore (academically). She understood that I had a learning disability but she never allowed me to use it as an excuse.

She reminded me that just because I was different, didn't mean that I was dumb. I became wiser before my time, when daddy wasn't around I had to quickly adapt to being one of the men of the house. I had to do my part in hopes that the boat wouldn't sink. She taught me how to survive, how to smile during turmoil, and the importance of keeping God first. My mother is a true businesswoman; she's the glue that holds everything together. She's who introduced me to love, which produces, patents, kindness, understanding, and more.

During the years of caring for her, I was blessed to sit under her wisdom, spiritual guidance, and her unique outlook on life. If my mother could birth six children, bury one and raise five, I'm sure that I can stay in good spirits knowing that my mother sees pass my face into my heart and soul.

- Your weakest moment is your strongest moment.

Wait   3/9/13@4:12am

I've graduated from college, built strong relationships at Warner Brothers, produced an impressive resume, PRAYED TO GOD, and applied to every job available. I have always made decisions that would place me in a position of power, which would give me the control of my outcome. But what do you do, when there is nothing else that you can do?

My temporary assignment at Warner Brothers ended 93 days ago, and I only have twenty dollars to my name. I have overdrawn all of my bank accounts and exhausted my credit card.

For the first time in my life I sit still, not knowing what to do next. Yesterday I saw the eviction notice taped to my neighbor's apartment door. It saddened me, but fear never entered my heart. WHENEVER YOU'RE WAITING ON GOD, IT FEELS LIKE YOU'RE WAITING FOREVER. The devil continues to taunt me, telling me to go back to Chicago because it would be so much easier. In my book giving up is so much harder than trying. Deep in my heart I know that this is where God has been strategically waiting to get me.

I feel myself standing right at the edge because I have ran out of resources, and the only one who can save me is him. A man without God is a disaster; he's the only lifeline that's keeping me sane. This is a very sensitive place for me, emotions are flaring and my temper is short. There is so much that I want to do but there is nothing that I can do.

I feel stuck. But then I am reminded that sometimes God has to break you down to build you up. I am reminded that God is known for luring you to a quiet desert; positioning you to LISTEN. I wonder if this is his way of saying that it's time to submit and commit. It brings joy to my heart when I think of all the great things that the creator has in store for me, however I soon become saddened when I question if I can be trusted.

Truth be told when times were good, I was so caught up with the hustle and bustle of life that I barely spoke to God; and when I did, the conversation lacked passion and sincerity. When a lamb departs from the flock and wonders into danger; the shepherd boy takes his rod, breaks it's legs, picks the lamb up and carries it until he heals. The animal not only learns not to leave the flock anymore, but it also learns to depend on the shepherd boy. I know for a fact that God has broken my legs.

It's apparent to me now that if I continue to put my agenda before his, he will continue to chastise until I submit and commit to his agenda.

There is much soul searching that must take place during the waiting process. Stop wasting time and energy crying and complaining. Focus on the survival lessons that are being taught which will help you during your journey through the wilderness. Transition your mind from your aspirations to what God desires you to learn during this significant moment.

God is simple, either you're going to be all in or all out. We make things complicated because we DON'T want to be faithful however we want all the perks. If you're reading this chapter in hopes to find an answer for your struggle, good luck; because I'm also praying to find an answer as I expose my scattered thoughts.

- Never measure a man by where he stands but instead, measure him from where he started.

The unseen Journey of a Genius March 10th@8:06pm

Flunking the second grade and being labeled a special ed student traumatized me. I didn't understand my disability therefore I accepted what others said about me. During my early years in college I quickly tried to transform into someone I wasn't; in hopes to create an acceptable identity. Others that knew me prior to college often tried to remind me of who I really was. It became frustrating because I didn't want to be that person anymore.

I remember my name quickly transforming from Don Davis into Donamechi the Genius. Say what you want but the name and the image became catchy and stuck. Now I had another issue, how do I keep up such a heavy title of a Genius? I remember the academic pressures being so extreme that I would immediately become exhausted. One night I stayed up late for hours studying, but nothing seemed to stick. This happened often therefore I felt like studying was a waste of time. However this moment was different, I never broke down and spazed out like this before.

I walked to the restroom livid, impatient, and full of rage. I stared and yelled at myself in the mirror, immediately becoming verbally abusive. "What the &#@% is wrong with you, you stupid BASTARD?" I quickly cut on the faucet and splashed water in my face. But being tired wasn't the reason I couldn't comprehend. I then took the palm of my hand and continuously slapped it against my forehead, as though that would solve the problem.

I guess I spaced out, because it was a while before I realize that my crying, yelling, and physical abuse woke my peers. They stood at the door staring at me. They looked at me with concern and disbelief, but I said nothing, as I dried my face, walked back to my room and continued to study. I became extremely hard on myself because I had three points to prove: #1 I belonged at Morehouse, #2 I was smart, and #3 I was strong enough to be an example for the youngsters in my family.

During my journey of finding self, I became stressed. It became difficult because I felt that if I was to become someone I was not, I first had to convince others that I was someone that I wasn't. My mother always tried to reinsure me that I was special, but it soon faded once I stepped back into an academic setting. Questions quickly appeared. How do I become whole when I'm so broken? How do I become the greatness that my mother says, dwells inside of me? How do I place my trust in the failure of my reflection every morning? How can a man look so strong and certain, but feels so insecure and weak? Last but not least, how can I have so many problems but I'm looked upon for the solution?

I remember when Charles Whitman (Actor) and I struggled in our business calculus class at Morehouse College. Day after day, the challenges disheartened us. After class we would sit in Charles car, lean back in our seats, and blast KANYE WEST "everything I'm not makes me everything I am." A mans struggles builds the character and zeal which produces a legend. Understand that who you are is preparation for who you're about to become. Monitor your growth. Be sure that bad situations produces greatness instead of allowing good situations to bring the worst out of you.

Genetics! 6/1/2013@3:45am

Around 6:00am my father's eyes slowly opened as he wiped his face and sat up on the edge of the bed. The late summer of 1966 was normal but on September 7th his life would immediately change forever. My mother continued to slumber as my father stood and headed to my older siblings room to check on them as usual. My father smiled as he glanced at my brother (Warren J. Davis Jr.) and my sister (Shiquita Davis) as they continued to sleep. However his smile quickly began to fade after he slowly turned and noticed Keisha stiff-arm that was raised above her face. He instantly knew she was dead.

When removing her arm from her face he quickly noticed the warm milk that traveled from out of his four-month-old daughters nose. My father was no stranger to death because he buried his mother four months prior. I asked my father what he felt at that exact moment and he responded by unselfishly saying that he didn't feel anything, his focus was on the reaction of his wife. He told me that the rooms were right next to each other but when having to tell his wife that their daughter is dead it quickly became the longest walk of his life.

My father slowly sat on the edge of their bed once again, this time facing my mother and slightly shaking her until she fully woke and said "Keisha is dead". My mother processed the dreadful information in a fraction of a second and her reality instantly became a nightmare that she couldn't wake from, as she repeatedly said "no Jeff, nooo.

"Fear snatched her core as her brain signaled her body to release adrenalin into her bloodstream. Her eye pupils began to dilate as the hairs stood on the back of her neck. If her skin was broken or slightly torn, the blood automatically coagulated (Thickened) to prevent blood lost.

Her chest expanded to increase the volume of inhaled air as the Bronchioles relaxed allowing greater amounts of oxygen to enter her lungs. Her heart quickly dilated while beating extremely faster, increasing the blood output. Her muscles began to contract as her blood pressure rose. Blood vessels near the surface of her skin tightened as well, causing her skin to become pale. My mother setup in the bed as she begged my father "bring me my baby."

My father fulfilled her request by bringing her the corpse. Rigor mortis had set in but the warmth from my mother's grip, while holding Keisha tightly against her chest made her body limp again.

Moments later, the paramedics arrived trying to pry the body from my mothers arms. They lied, by assuring my mother that they were not taking Keisha away, but they just wanted to make sure she was breathing properly instead. When my mother and father arrived to the hospital, it wasn't long before the doctor pronounced my sister's death.

Denial was the only thing that kept my mother calm while sitting in the waiting room. When my mother's denial was no longer an option the doctors had no choice but to drug her as she screamed for her baby. Preparing for her daughters funeral was torcher.

One would agree that my mother was losing her mind as she shopped for clothes that would keep my sister warm while Keisha laid to rest after the burial. My father didn't have the luxury of being hurt because my mother depended on all of his strength.

I asked my mother what it was that kept her from losing her mind and what made her keep going. She responded by saying "nothing but God, because I ran out of myself." I quickly remembered my auntie Dollie explaining the importance of the two tanks on her Peterbilt truck.

She told me that when exhausting one gasoline tank while traveling long distances the truck automatically pulls gas from the second tank which fuels the rest of the journey.

My mother adopted this mindset understanding that the mind can only do so much before breaking down under extreme amounts of pressure. However my mother depended on her spiritual connection as her second tank.

I know for a fact that GENETICS are strong, and even though you have not been placed in identical situations the power of GENETICS still exist. I have learned that you will know what you have when you recognize what you come from. Someone asked me what keeps me going and I responded by saying that its not me but it's the blood running through my veins.

- God is Unpredictable.

Orchestrated

I have been fasting until 5:00pm only eating one meal a day for months. Now that I think about it, there have been a number of days where I haven't eaten anything. Talking to God becomes my only comfort as my head starts ponding (massive headache), stomach growls, mouth becomes dry and a knot forms in my throat.

People continue to clearly inform me of my drastic weight loss but I continue to deny it. One of my friends that I have not seen in months told me that I looked sick. Truth is told; I am sick, I'm just sick of my situation, ready for it to change.

I'm no fool; I notice that the fat cells in my face and around my eyes are dissipating rapidly, giving me a sunken and hollowed appearance. However I am not discouraged because I still BELIEVE! I don't always hear him, nor feel him but I can see him clearly.

God is utilizing me as a pond during this game of life called chess, strategically positioning me while I anxiously anticipate the win. I have learned that God puts people in your path for a purpose. God has placed me in powerful circles since I have began this fast. Two years ago a friend of mine (Haven Finney) told me that he wanted to connect me with a guy by the name of DeVon Frankin. I had no idea who DeVon was and at that time I was so busy trying to get situated that my schedule didn't permit us to meet.

A year later my cozen Kimberly Scott-Eskridge advised me to read a book entitled Produced by faith by DeVon Frankin (VP @ Sony also Married to Megan Good). It took me 4 months to follow her advice but I finally did, and the book motivated me to connect and collect all the information that was available during my temp position as a floater at Warner Brothers.

The first brain I picked was of a young brother by the name of Daniel Ferguson (*Manager @ Warner Brothers*), which immediately became a great help when introducing me to Marco Williams (*Executive @ Warner Brothers*), Marco introduced me to Christopher Mack (*VP @ Warner Brothers*).

While working in the tour department I bumped into Drew Brown (*VP of Warner Horizon*). He quickly invited me to his office; Drew Brown was one of the coolest guys I ever met. His position was simple; he took part in giving the yes or no to any multimillion-dollar television show to air on national TV. Weeks later Daniel and I spoke again, after expressing my passion about service he soon introduced me to Andrea (*Executive Black Employees BRG @ Warner Bros*).

Weeks later Andrea and I saw each other at a NAMIC (*National association for multi-in communication*) event, which was held at Duane Martin & Tisha Campbell restaurant Xen, in California. Andrea was aware of my Major and introduced me to Jermaine Walton (*Sr. international Marketing Analyst @ Warner Brothers*) after laughing with Duane and Tisha.

Jermaine and I quickly became friends as he took me under his wings, helping me to become more marketable for the position that I desired. Jermaine quickly became impressed with me and introduced me to his boss, Don Polite (*VP of Warner Brother Marketing Dept.*) Don schooled me on the importance of building strong relationships and how hiring managers go with whom they know.

I was sure to ask intriguing questions, which turned a 30minute meeting into a 2hour meeting. The conversation was so good that he only took two bites of his salad.

He soon became impressed with who I was as a young man. He informed me to keep an eye open of any positions that may be available in his department.

A day later he forwarded my resume to Amy Chen (*Market recruiter @ Warner Brothers*), and Michael Rweyemamu (*VP of Sales for New Theatrical releases*). After our meeting I called and spoke with Jermaine, he told me to come into the office. Jermaine encouraged me by expressing how much of a great job that I have been doing by making such impressive connections. He advised me that from that day on whomever I sit and meet with I should ask for 3 contacts of friends in the industry that I can also sit and talk with.

I was in the game deep enough to allow the people that I met with to now work for me. He then asked a specific career path that I was interested in. My responses were scattered. He laughed and told me that I was all over the place.

He told me that if I could not narrow it down to 3 different fields at the most, recruiters wouldn't take me serious. He then told me that once I chose three totally different fields of work, which I could see myself pursuing.

After doing such my primary goal was to connect professionally and socially with people in those matching industries.

Jermaine continued by asking if I was booking or banking connection? I didn't understand the question so he explained. He said that banking connections are meeting people that you may need later. However on the other hand, booking is developing connections that you need now.

I responded by saying booking, and soon after he nodded his head while saying, "correct". Jermaine shared the importance of being prepared and organized while having an agenda of what will be discussed during a meeting. He continued by suggesting that I research (*social media, Google and more*) people before meeting with them. He told me that it is very important to find a common ground; this will help others remember you while making the process easier.

Jermaine Informed me to take heed of the fact that only 2% of assistants (*gatekeepers of the executives*) receive thank you cards. Last but not least he told me to never build all my relationship in only one company.

Jermaine told me to reach out and have coffee with people from different studios because the woman who hired him knew him prior WB, when she worked over at Sony. On my way I meditated on the valuable information that was given.

When I arrived at my apartment and checked my emails I became informed of an event the DeVon franklin was hosting but the tickets started at $250.00.

The event started at 7:30pm but I was sure to dress in my best arriving at 6:00pm. They allowed me to walk right in because they were not finished setting up an in addition I looked the part (*important*). I quickly sat, broke the ice with others and began mingling. I quickly noticed an African American male sitting by himself at a reserved table and went over to introduce myself. His name was Kweisi and he was from Chicago as well. We quickly exchanged information and we insured each other that we would keep in touch.

I continued to move around the room being sure to thank the bouncers at each door for helping us with the event (I had nothing to do with the event but now they thought I did) Just incase I wanted to invite friends. The night was coming to a close and I have yet to talk to DeVon. My friend Jason and his girlfriend Lauren finally arrived at the door. I quickly informed the bouncers that they were with me and he allowed them to enter. NOW my focus was back to meeting DeVon.

I asked God how I was to approach DeVon unlike any other, leaving a lasting impression? Just then Kweisi approached me, introducing me to a woman by the name of Tosha Whitten Griggs. Making small talk I asked her if she always lived California. She said no and then informed me that she lived a Atlanta Georgia for a few years. I told her that I went to college in Atlanta.

She asked where, and I responded, "Morehouse".

Her eyes lit up as she anxiously expressed that she went to Spelman, we hugged, and laughed as though we knew each other for years. After telling her how much of a pleasure it was meeting her she responded by asking if I wanted to meet DeVon. I jokingly questioned if she could set that up. She responded by saying that as his publicist she should be able to do something.

She then walked me over to him and introduced us. DeVon and I shook hands, joked, laughed and I assured him that I would give him a copy of my book the next time we crossed paths. I didn't ask him for anything however he told me to keep in touch (Hollywood talk). As I walked away I immediately became more impressed with God's strategic Orchestration than meeting DeVon. God has an interesting way of pulling the scattered pieces together producing and directing the Oscar award winning feature film of your life. I use to be frustrated, but I understand that these are the stories I will have to tell while one day sitting on Oprah Winfrey's couch.

- Follow the one worth following (leader) and one day you will become a leader.

Mentor (Big Brother)

Warren taught me at a young age that the GENDER is what defines a male. He continued by explaining that it's the developed and mature mind of a male that defines a MAN.

It's not the amount of power that a MALE has that makes him a MAN but instead its what the male DOES with the power he has which makes him a MAN. Real men rather give than take and in addition he rather love than hate.

A male is only concerned with self-growth, however a MAN is concerned with the growth of his community as well. Society has confused the minds of many but it takes a MAN to restore the order. Warren advised me to learn, and embrace the lessons that life teaches, because one day I will have to teach the lessons that life has taught. He often assured me that I would make mistakes, but in return my mistake will make me.

Warren advised me to acknowledge and resolve the hurtful baggage that life has stored on the shelves of my heart. He told me that I wouldn't overcome my problems by ignoring them; but instead I would mentally adjust and adopt the situations as the norm for my life. He advised me to be careful of the baggage that I inadvertently carried because it will surely affect the people that cross my path.

The man who taught me how to say eat when I was an infant now teaches me how to conduct myself as a man. I remember sitting in his car full of frustration and discouragement, expressing how much I didn't care and how much I just wanted to give up on life.

My brother allowed me to cry but he never allowed me to cry for long. He then stared deep into my eyes and told me that I didn't have the luxury of giving up, and I better start caring before he gave me something to care about.

I took his threats seriously because he always said what he meant and meant what he said. My brother never allowed me to cheat myself while on his watch. He's the only man I have ever known that consistently tried to give me what my father didn't (TIME). He's been apart of every minor and major decision of my life; he's always been supportive. My brother believed in me and saw things that I didn't see in myself.

I declined a job opportunity from Disney upon graduation from Morehouse because I didn't think I was smart enough. When sharing this with my mentor he told me to shut up and take the job. He informed me to Follow my first mind, never second-guess my instinct; this is truly a God given gift.

It's almost impossible and inhuman to lie to self. Many times our ego leads us to our own demise. In every hurtful condition the red flag waved but your ego chose to ignore and depend on time, and the approval of others to show and tell you that you're wrong.

He told me that Its coward to call your own gut feeling a liar. He warned me to stop hoping to be wrong jus because I don't want to face disappointment.

Life is interesting, I remember as a teenager my brother would, advise me to always where a white t-shirt under a white dress shirt because it would make it brighter. He taught me the importance of perception and reminded me that people judge me by what they see. He reminded me to always keep my nails, hair and teeth up to part.

My mentor was always hard on me because he knew that life would be harder. He told me to learn from his mistakes but as I stated above he also understood that I had to make my own. Rich or Poor, guilty or innocent, I would always be his little brother.

He never failed to protect me; in addition he always tried to reduce the pain that I was sure to experience. He loved me so much that my hurt became his pain. My mentor gave me everything that he could and all he wanted in return was for me to be happy.

When it came to girls my brother told me to be careful, because when pursuing someone who is pursuing someone, my good deeds will easily be over looked.

Warren informed me that my life could easily become difficult by the woman who I marry. In addition he advised me to play my part when married. He warned me that a broken home and the lack of parenting alter a child's life/role.

I listened as he said "THROUGH MY FATHER MY BROTHER HAS BECOME MY ENEMY THOUGH MY MOTHER MY BROTHER HAS BECOME MY SON AND THROUGH MY PARENTS, I WAR WITH MYSELF". He reminded me that the person that I marry would be a partial reflection of our child.

He told me everything that he knew in hopes to prepare me during this journey called life. However The Master (My Father) showed me everything I needed to see, to prepare me for this journey called life.

- Running from your past may result to you arriving at your destiny

The Master (My Father)

The master has inadvertently inflicted much pain on me, which produced perfections that probably wouldn't have been possible if it wasn't for the extreme fiery experiences that slowly burned, and separated me from the impurities of life. Speaking in my father's defense I must tell the story like it is. My situation was different than some, I grew up with a strong hate for my father because I felt as though my father's loyalty to the streets was stronger than his loyalty for his son. I remember being hungry, sitting in our dark and cold house wondering where my father was, because I hadn't seen him in almost a year. The next day he appeared, the refrigerator was filled and all the utilities were immediately cut back on.

This told me that we were not poor; but instead my father didn't care. He would promise me that he wouldn't drink again and every time he promised, I believed him with all my heart, only to be let down again. I became angry with my oldest brother (warren) for chastising me and taking the role of my father, which soon produced division amongst siblings. I was too young to understand that my brother had sacrificed what he wanted (Being a Brother) for what I needed (A father figure) in hopes to make up for what my father lacked. But my father wasn't always like that.

My father is a PURE GENIUS in his field as a MASTER electrician. My father should be a multimillionaire by now, and where real estate is concerned, if you can name it, he probably owned it, but if he didn't, that does not mean that he couldn't afford it. My father was, and still is brilliant, handsome, full of charm, and very sure of his craft. Many admired my father. He spent a lot of time with my older siblings and while at work he sacrificed his health, his hand, and even his life to provide for his family.

But where did he go wrong? People often overlook the power of an addiction. My father felt as though he could control the substance, however it ended up controlling him. To be honest I don't know which was worst, watching him drink or watching the withdrawal process. My father would drink for months at a time; therefore his body relied on alcohol. Alcohol is a depressant that acts like a sedative or tranquilizer. When the intake of alcohol is suddenly stopped, the body may go into shock, quickly causing withdrawal.

I would sit quietly; watching my father clench his stomach, as his hands shook uncontrollably. I would watch as he vigorously bit his bottom lip, while his body broke into a cold sweat. His breaths became short as tears rolled down his face. At the tender age of eight I continued repeating myself, "Are you okay daddy?" and he would respond, "I'm going to be okay big boy." He never wanted me to see him in such condition; therefore he continued to tell me to leave the room. But I never did, I stayed, because I didn't want him to feel the loneliness that I felt, when he abandoned me.

Please believe me when I say "the bad time were bad, however the good times were good." When my parents separated for a while he would get my brother (Shawn) and I on the weekends and take us to the pancake house, letting us order anything we wanted. As a kid I always had a million questions and my father always had a million answers. My dad worked long and hard hours, however he was never too tired to spend time with my brother and I.

At this time my parent's marriage was very unhealthy. As crazy as it may sound they always argued about the same thing, he drank too much and she shopped too much. As dysfunctional as my household was it didn't bother me because it was all that I knew.

There were many times that my dad could do no wrong where I was concerned. During his sober moments my dad was a great provider and a strong father. In all actuality my father was my IDOL, I guess that's why I disliked him so much, for allowing alcohol to take my HERO away from me. During my older years I asked my mother if my father had always been a heavy drinker.

She responded by saying "NO" and that his drinking began after his mother died. If you seek for the reason, you will understand the action. My mentor (brother) informed me that my father's, father was an alcoholic and that my pops didn't have much of an influential role model. My dad fended for himself, moving from Oklahoma to Chicago and quickly became a man before the age of fourteen.

He would spend the whole day chasing golf balls in hope to make enough money to feed his mom, siblings & him-self. Later in life he met a man by the name of T.Baby who equipped him with a trade, which would be utilized to provide for my dad and his future family to come.

As I have grown older I notice that my dad and I operated by the same success system entitled trial and error. No one gave my father the directions to success, however that did not stop him from searching for it. My father did the best that he could, with what he had.

I was able to release the anger when God allowed me to acknowledge the difference between my father and his addiction. Once I release the anger I released myself from being captive.

The best advise my father gave me was to get a grip on life while I'm still young because if I don't I will become content with mediocrity.

My father acted like a "know it all", until the day that I became old enough to act like a "know it all", and when becoming a reflection of my father I noticed that he didn't know much at all.

My daddy had an internal struggle trying to step out of himself with a plea trying to become the man that I needed to see, in hopes that it would be the man that I was willing to be.

If someone were to ask who I am, the response would be simple. I am the best of my family and friends, mixed with many of my own mistakes and insecurities.

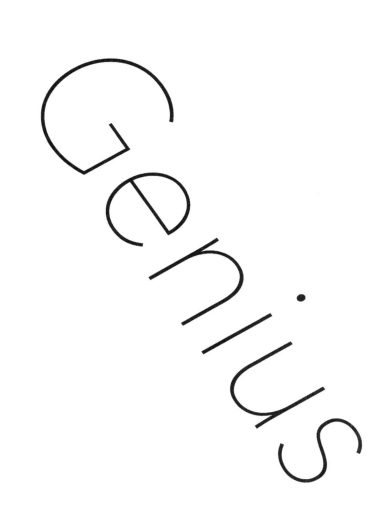

- If you go against the grain, ruffle a few feathers, and push the envelope. I promise that you will be remembered.

Frustration-April 6th 2013

I arrived at Hally Berry's gala forty minutes late. When sitting at the Warner Brothers table the Vice President of Warner Bros writing program and I quickly noticed one another. I knew we would cross paths once again. However I am sure that he wasn't looking forward to it. The last time we spoke, he asked me about my life story, I informed him of my struggle, and he told me to send him my resume. I sent my resume, followed up, and for weeks I waited, but there was no response.

My temp position at Warner Brothers has been over, however the company is so big that no one noticed that I was relieved of my position, months ago. He leaned over and shook my hand. I didn't even try to crack a smile because I wanted him to feel the negativity, and frustrated energy that ran through my veins.

Trying to make small talk he asked how I was doing, I responded by telling him that I was alive. At this moment his position (VP) didn't impress me; it just made things worst. He then asked me if I still worked at Warner Bros, I responded by telling him that I have not worked since I sent him my resume. He then asked me what I was doing for money.

I honestly don't think he understood how inappropriate that question was. However I told him that I try my best to hide my struggles behind a suit and a smile. He then told me if I needed anything to let him know. The phony gesture DISTURBED me, and it immediately seemed impossible to compose myself. I swiftly leaned in and told him that I only needed one thing from him, and that's a job, but if he wouldn't deliver, then I am fine with hello. He slowly leaned back in his seat, gathered his thoughts, stood up, and excused himself from the table in order to go to the restroom.

Anger hid behind my smile, because as the VP, (*making almost a half a $ million annually*), he had the power to grant me an opportunity. Or at least give me an internship, which would allow me to earn a position. But instead he continued to BS me with kind gestures that he knew that he wouldn't hold up to. I kept trying to humble myself by thinking spiritually, understanding that it was a privilege that God allowed me to sit at a table fully paid for, surrounded by VP's and executives from Warner Bros who all knew me by name. But on this day the natural over threw the spiritual as I continued to ponder on the fact that I was so close but so far from my goal.

Moments later the food was served, and God knows I was starving. I was dressed like a millionaire, however I only had four dollars to my name that sat in my right pocket. This was my first and only meal of the day therefore I was careful to eat slow, not provoking any extra attention to self.

I sat in a room full of famous celebrities and wealthy producers however it meant nothing because their success wasn't mine.

 A few days later the executive director from the board in which I sat on, emailed my personal account and asked me if I still worked for Warner Brothers. She told me that she noticed my Warner Bros email address was canceled. I replied with the truth telling her that I have not worked in months. Her response is that she would have to let me go from the board because I was no longer an employee. Now what do I do? This kills my all access to the Warner Brothers lot and the exclusive events allowing me to show my face and network, which helps to build stronger relationships. Once again I'm lost.

I found myself taking a long hot bath and laying across the bed talking to God in the middle of the day. My mind began to race so fast that I immediately became exhausted. I woke up hours later and immediately saw a missed call from my mother. I called back, she asked me what was wrong; I told her that I didn't know what to do anymore. She reminded me that the waiting process means wait. She questioned if I was going to stress about the situation or pray, and in addition she told me that I had to choose one because I could not do both.

My mother told me that faith and fear is like oil and water, it doesn't mix. Life is interesting, you only have what God built you with and that's all you need to succeed in life.

My mother told me to stop insulting God by asking him for minute things. I had the tendency of asking God for things that seemed possible. She reminded me that God is a big God; therefore he is capable of doing big things. I soon adopted her mindset and that's when I became free from the fear of disappointment. I began talking differently, understanding the power of words. We have what we have because we speak life into what we have when we complain.

I told my mother that I have faith in God but I also feel defeated. She responded by saying "defeat is only temporary, don't let it become a state of mind." My mother continued by saying, "have faith, pray about it and forget it because it's all apart of God's plan. For the first time in almost a year I had no professional ties to Warner Brothers and it bothered me.

My mother told me that there must be a disconnection before a new connection can take place. She reminded me that when things seem like they are falling apart they might actually be falling in place. My mother warned me to become careful not to focus on the natural (my will) but instead, focus on the spiritual (Gods Will) because if I focused on the natural I will quickly become impatient with the process.

My mother advised me to stop focusing on Warner Brothers and start focusing on the fact that God is preparing me for something bigger.

I still question what that something is, but I honestly feel as though he will reveal it soon. The two reasons that I worked so hard to sustain a position at Warner Bros is because it would offer financial stability while allowing me to break into the industry.

My mother quickly reminded me that God is my provider who utilizes Warner Brothers as a tool to finance my lifestyle. Now that I think about it she was telling me the truth, because my temp position only paid $10 an hour before taxes and in most cases I wouldn't even work 48 hour weeks.

My rent here in California is $956.00 a month. God recently allowed Bank Of America home loans to grant my modification which granted me the opportunity to keep my four bedroom home in Chicago while reducing my mortgage from $1,200 to $450 a month.

The interesting part is that I didn't even mention my utilities for both places, cell phone bill $130.00), nor food and fuel for my car to sustain my travels throughout the month.

Wow, how long does it take for us to notice? And in addition look at how fast we forget? Once again I owe God an apology because I stress, wonder, and worry about what I don't have when in all actuality I should be thanking him for giving me everything that I need.

- Be wise, young one, because one moment in time can change your entire future.

He saved me

In 2011 I watched the news around 12:40 p.m, while getting dressed for a meeting that I had in LA. While watching, I noticed that 26-year-old Tyler Brehm opened random fire around 10:19 a.m. and sadly murdered music executive John Atterberry. I stood numb and cold, staring at the television when they showed the location of the murder. If it was not for the fact that I just got my car shipped to California I would have left for my meeting hours earlier, inadvertently arriving to the murder scene at 9:50a.m.

Sitting and waiting on the next bus which would take another 45 minutes. I knew the rout because I traveled it weekly. I would take the north Hollywood train to Vine street, then I would walk a few blocks down, in order to wait on the 210 bus which would take me to West Angeles Church.

In 2010 I found myself at a club sitting in VIP with a group of associates that I met at the resort which were also from America. It was my first time in the Dominican Republic and so far I was having a ball. The women in the DR are beautiful and in addition they are attracted to Americans because they think that we're rich.

I could barely walk through the club because women continually pulled on me trying to catch and keep my attention. Truth is told, their ultimate goal is to get a green card in hopes to move from their impoverished situation. The night soon came to an end and everyone chose a woman and took them back to the hotel. I purposely walked out solo however a beautiful woman quickly caught my attention and asked if she could walk with me. I granted her request and allowed her walk back to the resort with me.

She wore a colorful bracelet that gave her access to the resort, it was odd to me then, but it makes since to me now. We had great conversation as we arrived to my hotel door. I gave her a hug and told her that I hoped to see her around. When closing the door she quickly knocked on it. I slowly opened the door to a beautiful smile, and she softly asked to come in, in hopes to keep me company. She had long silky brown hair that touched her behind; she stood 5'4 and weighted about 135 pounds.

Her body was shaped to perfection and I could not stop staring in her stone grey eyes. We both stood, gazing at one another in silence as she boldly griped my crotch area. God knows I wanted to slowly undress her but the truth is, I didn't have a condom and a baby would have surely come from this deal. I had no chose but to reject her request by apologizing and reminding her that it was getting late. She asked for a kiss goodnight. I said sure, and to her surprise I kissed her on her forehead instead of her lips. I went to sleep mad at myself for passing up such a memorable opportunity. The next night I sat, laughing and joking at a lounge with some Americans and a few DR locals that I knew. Time quickly passed and our eyes quickly connected as she walked in. We smiled at each other but we acted as though we didn't know each other as I watched her sit in VIP with he friends. I told one of the guys that I sat next to that she was the one that I had to have sex with before I left the Dominican Republic.

He grew up in the DR and it seemed as though he knew everyone. He responded by saying whom, I pointed and said her. I watched as his smile soon faded as he warned me to stay away from her. I curiously asked why. He responded by informing me that she had aids. Death stood at my bedroom door and I didn't even know it.

In 2009 @ 2:45am, I found myself in California on the 405 (expressway), racing against my close friend Charles Whitman (Famous & Brilliant Actor) exceeding the limits of110 mph. He was in an Infinity truck and I drove a 2010 Mercedes Benz, while blasting ICE CREAM PAINT JOB by DORROUGH MUSIC. I held the steering wheel with my left hand, while gently gripping Lemans inner thigh with my right hand. Her and I met at the club moment's prior as strangers, but we headed to my hotel as though we were a couple. The next morning the rental car company called me and asked me to bring the car in immediately.

When I arrived they apologized and switched the car out for another Benz. I asked the gentleman the problem and he told me that they mistakenly gave me the wrong car. He continued by telling me that the Benz that I had, was being worked on.

After walking around the car he secretly informed me that the nuts which were used to secure the wheels to the car were extremely loose and he told me that it was a blessing that I didn't take the 405, because it's a great chance that the wheels could have come off. He apologized again telling me that if he had known the condition, he would have sent a flat bed tow truck to come pick it up.

During the summer of 2007 Mr. James, my oldest brother, and I was remodeling a house in Ford Heights Illinois when two teenagers attempted to rob us by aiming guns in our faces. But that wasn't the first time I had a gun pointed in my face. In 2006 someone hit the car of a friend of mines at the time, Barell Morgan's therefore Cliff, Lerrick, Barell and I jumped in Cliffs truck and chased the guy down.

When cutting him off we all jumped out of the truck. For some strange and odd reason I was the one who walked up to the car first. To my surprise the driver pulled out a gun and pointed it at me out of fear. Fear never entered my body as I stared down the barrel of his gun. Please believe that it wasn't because I was tuff but it was because it all happened so fast.

A Pure Genius

If I had one wish, it would be to capture the laughter of the naysayers on audio, with the intention of playing it back to myself repeatedly. As a youngster I remember expressing my ideas to others, and in return no one believed me, in fact they thought that I was insane. I heard Dame Dash (Producer and the co-founder of Roc-A-Fella Records) say that it's common for a genius to lose his/her mind. When one loses his/her mind they are diagnosed as being insane.

The definition of genius is one of exceptional intellectual or creative power or other natural ability. "Insanity is doing the same thing over and over again and expecting different results. I find it to be fascinating that a person who's considered to be a genius or insane does not know his/her mental state until someone else makes them aware of it.

It's fascinating that neither geniuses nor the insane ever believe what the doubters see. There is a language and a belief barrier that separates the insane from the sane. They say that an insane man is disturbed, but truth is, an insane man does not care to be disturbed by the doubts of life. Those who can't do, nor see your vision will try to discourage you by labeling you a misfit.

The insane have no boundaries therefore it is impossible for he/she to process the word no. Perception plays a big part when it comes to being a genius. You are what you perceive because what you perceive is what you believe. To change your thoughts, you must first change your perception. One must also understand that perception is brought in by the human nervous system (Bodies function that interprets, store and respond to Information from the inside and out).

Others may see the glass as half empty but you see it as half full. The true genius lies NOT in acknowledging the building after it has been built, but appreciating it while its being constructed.

A real genius believes in his/her divine and direct spiritual connection, which guides them in their purpose. You're no fool; you know that others secretly doubt your capability. They think you fell off! But truth be told your silence is needed during the preparation of changing the game" In our silence we hear GOD the loudest, allowing us to visualize the Playbook and execute it in the game! Get use to hearing no, and understand that many will doubt you.

According to aeronautical science, bumblebees can't fly. It's said that the ratio of his wingspan to the size of his body makes flying totally impossible. The bumblebee, who is ignorant such technical matters continues to fly anyway. As I encourage you, I encourage myself; they may call you insane today but you will surely go down in history as a Genius tomorrow.

Experiences produced who I am.

Survival 4/20/13 @ 2:22a.m.

Never say what you'll never do, and never sit so high where you can't sympathize with someone else's lows. I've been discouraged, lost, hurt, hungry, and homeless; therefore I had to learn this lesson the hard way. I never thought I would sell my clothes, pawn my jewelry, retrieve aluminum from the public trashcans nor eat a stranger's leftovers. I know for a fact that life has cheated me however God has never mistreated me.

I have learned that once survival mode occurs, the thin line of ethics soon disappears. Two days ago I wanted to go to bible study @ West Angeles Church, where I volunteered every Wednesday. The issue that I faced was the fact that I only had a five-dollar bill and eight dollars on my capital one credit card. With an empty tank, I knew that thirteen dollars wouldn't get me back and forth from church and afford me something to eat. I was left with no choice but to do what the old folks would do, and that's press my way.

When arriving at the corner gas station I swiped my card at the pump. I was knowledgeable enough to know that when the machine senses that there are some funds available, it will allow you to pump as much gas as needed.

I used this opportunity to fill my tank, knowing that I would get hit with an overdraft fee. However I had payment protection on my credit card therefore my insurance would pick up the monthly minimum payment and the overdraft fee.

Church was good as usual but before leaving Brian Bradley asked if I could help him take some bibles back to his office. Unaware of my situation he stuffed forty dollars in my hand. This was more than a blessing because I had no idea of how I would eat that night, nor the next day. The day before that my cell phone bill was due ($145.00) and God knows I didn't have the money. I needed my phone because I was waiting on calls about employment opportunities. I called the phone company and lied, telling them that I have had poor service with them for over a month and there must be a tower down in the area. To my surprise, it was a tower down, and the lady was kind enough to erase my whole balance.

 Not to long before that Donnie Briggs and I was driving, and he asked me to pull over so he could get some money out of the ATM. When getting back into the car he stuff $100 in my hand. I knew it was God because no one knew how desperate my situation was. My tricks of pulling up in fast-food windows, complaining about an order that I never placed are coming to an end.

I can no loner write bad checks from one back account and manually deposit them into another bank account in hopes that I can pull out additional funds from the ATM before the system notices that the checks are bad. No longer can I report my debit card stolen, after disguising myself while at grocery stores exhausting my Bank Of America card, careful not utilize my normal signature when purchasing food. This is a difficult moment of survival for me, because I have to quietly depend on other people's obedience to God.

I have no means of income and I have no idea what tomorrow may bring. God has sat me in a seat where I depend on him more than I depend on myself. This is a miserable stage for me because I have always been a giver, a lender, a leader, and in control. I feel like a charity case and no matter how hard I try, it seems impossible to pull myself out of this ditch. I have pulled myself from deeper situations than this, this is how I know that God is keeping me, calming me, teaching me, and building me. The prideful part of me says that I don't want anyone doing anything for me because I don't want to be reminded of it later.

The wisdom embedded inside of me says, "how do you allow a friend to prove his friendship if you continues to deny him from his duties?" I agree that it's difficult when you're not able to carry your own. You could have an issue with pride, ego, control and more. But I advise you to learn how to give when God allows you to give; and receive when God places you in a position to receive.

Please remove self-emotion and learn from my mistakes, because if you don't God will apply the pressure that will make you learn.

- Stop coloring in the lines and create your own

John 4/30/13@ 2a.m.

Lately I have been "lost in my own space" (*Warren J Davis Jr.*). No direction just knowing that time continues to pass. For the first time in my life I have blocked out everything as I sat quietly in the corner of my room. While in deep prayer and meditation for direction, an email that Tamera Love (*friend that works for E! network*) sent me crossed my mind. The email read, "You Don't Need a Job".

God then reminded me of one of my major goals (*to buyout or create my own distribution company*). Later that day I arrived at John Singletons (*famous Movie Director*) tribute that was held by the DGA African American screening committee. The first time I met John was in June 2009 back stage at the BET (*Black Entertainment Television*) music awards.

I tried to give him my newly published book (I Am Loyal) in hopes that he would read it and give me some feed back in the near future. John Singleton refused to take the book because of legal purposes (Displaying my content on film without my permission could get him sued).

However he saw that I was persistent and wrote his office address on a piece of paper, agreeing to give me thirty minutes of his time. When arriving to the address the next day, the security guard chuckled when observing my overt confidence, and assured me that John has not had an office space there in years. I pulled away in disbelief, full of discouragement and frustration.

But that wasn't the first or the last time I was lied to nor laughed at by a Hollywood legend. In 2006 Spike Lee (Famous Filmmaker) came to Morehouse campus and I was sure to ditch all my classes with the intentions of following him around with a five-page treatment for a new movie.

He refused to take it and I refused to be refused. Later that day out of frustration he took the treatment from my hand and began reading it. Moments later Spike looked at me in disbelief and suggested that I should first turn it into a novel before he helped me turn it into a feature film.

I was inspired to write a novel and in addition I was sure to tell all my friends and even the girl who I was dating at the time that Spike Lee assured me that once I finished the novel we would make it a feature. Everyone laughed at me, but I didn't care, young and gullible, I knew Spike was telling me the truth.

It wasn't until a year later, while sitting in Belize at an old ran down dinner table writing my book that I realized that Spike never read the treatment. In fact he only read the cover page, which only provided my name and contact information.

I laughed at myself because in addition to that I immediately noticed that we never exchanged contact information. However when I published the book (I Am Loyal) I found his address on his website and sent him a copy, I have yet to hear anything until this day. But nothing beats my experience in the lower level parking garage of the Phillips Arena in Atlanta GA, during the JAY Z and MARY J BLIGE concert.

Charles Whitman (Famous Actor and Friend) and I were walking when we immediately noticed Tyler Perry (Famous Filmmaker) and his friend walking to his car. We quickly walked up to them and introduced ourselves however we were rudely interrupted by a peddler who was trying to sell Tyler Perry a bootleg movie. Charles and I continued to follow Tyler to his car as the man continued to harass him. Finally the peddler gave up as Tyler approached his car.

I quickly asked Tyler Perry for a few minutes of his time and he responded by saying that he had to go. While opening his door right before jumping in his red Ferrari I said "Tyler give me a few minutes man, you cut me short".

Tyler Perry laughed and replied by saying "I ain't cut you short, your mama and daddy cut you short". I couldn't do nothing but watch him shut the car door as he revved up his loud engine and quickly pulled off while I stood there watching. Charles looked at me and said " I will never support another one of his movies again in my life". I thought Charles was just momentarily frustrated, but he meant every word that came from his mouth.

Charles and I always laugh about that moment, even until this day. We consider it just another story we will have to tell when we sit on Oprah Winfrey's couch. I always asked God to give me strength and the patience to deal with the people when my time comes. Now that I'm older I understand that Tyler Perry was just being humorous; however my struggles didn't afford me the luxury of having such a personality at that exact moment.

Through the years I have had my fair share of shaking hands, my only request is to one day know what it feels like to be on the other end of that handshake. My experiences have prepared me to deal with people from all walks of life. During the Jon Singleton tribute my mothers words continued to echo in my ear "If you dress the part, and act the part, people will believe that you belong".

I have not worked for Warner Bros in months however when celebrities asked where I worked; guess what I told them?

You're dog on right; I told them that I worked for Warner Bros, in distribution. They thought I meant the distribution department for feature films. In all actuality I use to work in the distribution building for DVD's however I spent majority of my time on the main floor working in the VIP TOUR department as a greeter. But they didn't know that.

If you ever live in LA, its one thing that you should know; in most cases the first two questions that pops up is "what is your name", and "what do you do?" I hate to say it but these two questions will dictate how far your conversation will go. People don't waste time talking to anyone because they have a great personality. In the film industry it's about what you can do for them that keeps their interest. I knew a nice circle of people who worked at Warner Bros therefore the name game would only benefit me because I could back up everything that I said.

People are visual therefore I arrived early, dress as though I was wealthy, sat by the VIP check in counter, and crossed my legs while reading a paper. An older woman by the name of Alicia (*DGA Board worker*) sat next to me while saying hello. I responded with a smile however for the first few seconds I made it seem as though I had a greater interest in the paper as my eyes quickly returned to the article. As I predicted she asked my name and my profession. After talking for a while I quickly found out that we knew some of the same people.

She quickly introduced me to her supervisor and her supervisor introduced me to Oz Scott (*the co-chair of the DGA African American Steering Committee*). Oz was impressed with me and asked if I would join him in the VIP area for a bite to eat. 30 minutes later our surroundings quickly changed. Oz introduced me to Bill Dukes (Famous Director). Bill and I quickly found a common ground when talking about politics and the state of black film.

Bill introduced me to Ice Cube (*Music/Film maker*). I told Ice cube that Drew Brown (*VP of production at Warner Bros*) and I was just talking about him the other day. Cube smiled and told me to be sure to tell Drew that he said hello. AJ Johnson (*Famous Actress*) went to one of my sister colleges (*Spelman*) so when we embraced I reminded her from the several times we met prior. The VIP area quickly became pack as Taraji P. Henson (*Famous Actress*) and I stood shoulder to shoulder. Its sad to say but the game of networking in LA is simple.

Don't act like you're in need and people will get on board. I learned that only a few blacks in Hollywood has real money, the rest are just actors. In most cases its not that these people don't want to help you, the truth is that they can barley help themselves.

They keep you at a distance because the closer you become the quicker you will realize that they don't have anything but a little fame left.

Jon Singleton and I crossed paths several times that night, I know for a fact that he's one of the African Americans in Hollywood who really has it. I sat in my seat as the tribute to Jon Singleton began.

I couldn't stop smiling as I thought to myself "these people have no idea of who I am about to become". During the tribute people continued to say the same thing; JOHN opened the doors for them that no one else would open. One of the actors reminded us of the struggles that blacks have where getting decent movie roles are concerned. I heard her loud and clear because the truth was shallow in her tongue.

Jews and white boys are running Hollywood and in addition they dictate the images displayed on the big screen that plays into the stereotypes created to disrespect and discredit the value of our ancestors. Truth be told, majority of your well-paid celebrities are Caucasians. She made a point when she said that black actors only get one major role every other year and majority of the black actors who get a chance are recycled and tight cast. Her words were conformation; at that exact moment I was no longer "lost in my own space" (Warren J. Davis Jr.) because **Don Davis Distribution** was mentally founded.

- Call me ignorant! Because I have no idea what no means.

5/5/13 @ 1:32 a.m.

My philosophy is simple; if you want it, go get it. "I thought it, I spoke it, I did it, and it happened" (Donamechi Davis). Focusing on your obstacles triggers fear that immediately defeats you from conquering your goal, before you try. I heard someone say, "Life is an unscripted movie". If that's the case, I have plenty room for creativity. As an author I am wise enough to understand that I'm creative because I am connected to the creator, and his love, truth, and inspiration is what breathes LIFE into my creation. If you distance yourself from the creator it disturbs the connection that produces the creativity.

Speaking of pursuing what you want, I recently bumped into a beautiful woman at a wholefoods grocery store in Sherman oaks CA. I asked her for her name and inquired where she was from. She smiled while telling me that her name was Tatyana and that she was from New York. In addition she told me that she lived in California for years, and that she considers it to be her home. I asked if she would show me around since I was still kinda new in town. She smiled and politely refused my request; we shook hands and went our separate ways. I walked away knowing that Tatyana Marisol Ali (*Will Smith Co-Star/Fresh Prince of Bel-Air*) had no idea of who I was, or who I was soon to become; but I am convinced that one day she will.

Even though I had three more hours to go I couldn't wait to eat; my head was pounding and my stomach was starving. It's been months; but I have yet to give up my Daniel Fast until God blesses me with a career job. Moments after walking into my home I received a phone call from Trezanay M. Atkins, founder of TMA (the brand infringement firm). She offered me some legal advise about my company **Don Davis Distribution**. She advised me to cancel the meeting that I had with DeVon Franklin (*Executive at Sony*) and reminded me that I should never share my ideas with anyone who has more money and more resources than I do, until my ideas are legally secured.

However I ended up bumping into Devon two days later at a church function that he spoke at and we conversed for over a half an hour while standing in front of his all black sports addition Range Rover. I gave him a copy of my book (**I Am Loyal**) and my audio book (**A Journey to forgiveness**) and told him to check it out in his free time. I was careful not to discuss Don Davis Distribution with him however I did assured him that I would call him as soon as I finished the legalities of a project that I was working on.

I Tried to give them A Chance, to aboard my Vision

Don't expect people to understand your grind when God didn't give them your vision.
As I walked down the stairs, I immediately saw Damien Dante Wayans to my left traveling up the escalator. He was dressed incognito with a hoody and tennis shoes on, prepared for an intensive workout at the Sherman oaks Galleria's 24hour fitness (*gym in California*). I kept my cool; my approach was subtle as I said what up to him in the men's locker-room.

We're around the same age so there were no needs to give him an executive pitch. I congratulated him on his television show (*New Generation Wayans*) as an introduction for dialog about **Don Davis Distribution**. He thought that I was crazy to have an idea of competing against Warner Bros, Lions Gate, Sony, and Fox. He reminded me that I have yet to even make a movie or at least own a production company. Soon afterward I gave him my information and told him that we should meet because I wanted him to be a partner of my distribution company, he question why he should meet with someone who isn't known in the film industry or have yet to make at least a million dollars.

I asked him if a million dollars defines how valuable or creative a man is. He smirked and said "no", however it still wasn't enough to make him commit to meeting with me. After thirty minutes of his silence while listening to me rant passionately about how I was going to change the film industry, he smiled while telling me to stay encouraged. He saved my number in his phone and warned me that many people will tell me "no" however it's important to never hold grudges, and never become that bitter Ni##@ on the side line, mad because no one will let me in. We shook hands and went our separate ways as I continued saying to myself "Never be the bitter Ni#%@ on the side line, mad because no one will let me in."

•   Exposure, The Scattered thoughts

Submit and commit 6/6/13@8:28 p.m

Charles Whitman reminded me that I should never compare my success to someone else's because I don't know what he or she compromised to get where they are. It's difficult to watch your peers prosper when your life is stagnate, but it's worst when they're dominating the career/field that you've always wanted to be a part of. Neither jealousy nor envy has ever entered the heart, however the immediate tendency is to first question yourself (where did I go wrong, and what am I lacking?), in hopes that your self-evaluation will give you the answer, but instead, it produces more questions.

I eagerly raised my hand in a room of well over 100 Harvard students, while trying to learn from others mistakes; I was forced to ask the panel "what do you know now that you didn't know at my age, that if you had of known your life would have been different?" I watched as the eighty-year-old woman motioned that she would take the question. She sat there in silence for a moment trying to conger up the most elaborate answer she could find. The room adapted to her silence as we waited with our pen pressed to our pads, knowing that her words would be life changing therefore we were prepared to hold her answer dear to our hearts. Moments passed and I watched her slowly open her mouth and respond, "I would have went hard".

I was shocked by her choice of words. She continued by informing me that she had always been naturally smart and retaining information was very easy. She admitted that she entered the gates of Harvard because of who her father knew and reminded me that the international game of who you know is still played until this day. She continued by saying that she was lazy minded and became content with the statuesque. However her past haunts her present, because she will never know her full potential. She honestly admitted that there are many things that she wishes that she could do to change that, but her body has aged where it won't allow her to do so. She became silent again before repeating herself "I would have went hard". This reminds me that there are no sick days or pity parties when it comes to the marathon, you either give your all or go home!

Contradiction

There is pain in hunger that water can't fill and a void for love that sex will never thrill. People are everywhere but I'm walking alone. I have traveled so far mentally that I have lost the direction of my home. Tears have become common, as my heart has turned cold. Bad decisions have aged me and experiences have given me an old soul. People have betted against me and the wages are hi, I didn't even believe in myself this I can't lie. But I found perfection through my imperfection this lesson was hard, but this lesson came after much hurt while being delt a hand of bad cards.

God had to remind me that **I am a DIAMOND in the DIRT**. A mastermind built me so I must continue my masterwork. Mentally limited, I question my master "will I be fairly compensated for my journey" as though I'm defending myself and he's no longer my attorney. I asked him why he designed me with so many imperfections. He quickly responded by saying that it's my imperfections that makes his creation (me) a masterpiece.

As I get older my heart grows colder, out of fright, and I feel a conviction in the contradictions of life. I fight until my last breath is still, in hopes to conquer a world that's not real. I chase what I think I need, as though I am famished, and need a meal, knowing that what I want can easily kill. I struggle to live right in hopes that I will make it to heaven. However, no matter how good or bad I live, it won't guaranty a resting place in heaven.

True life comes after death, this I can't lie but isn't it odd that no one wants to die. It's interesting that a persons 10% of wrong doing can easily out weigh their 90% of kindness. I have a quick temper and I flirt with the dangers of life even faster, knowing that it can easily become my own disaster.

She's full of disappointment but I continue to lye at her doorstep. I find it interesting that a drunken talk exposes a sober mind. We ask God for wealth but in all actuality we're asking God to become less dependent of him. You thought I was different but truth be told I'm just like the rest of them.

- Exposure, The Scattered thoughts

JUAN 7/9/2013@ 11:22pm N-Chicago

Those who you love will be the ones who will be capable of hurting you the most. It's interesting that you can choose your FRIENDS however FAMILY is already chosen for you. Saving those that don't want to be saved (don't want to change for the better) would cause you to sink.

Love will make you feel obligated to help love ones who don't want to listen, nor help themselves. Logic tells you that you can only motivate others to do better, but they are the only ones who can make up their mind to save themselves.

Remember that the journey produces the struggle and the struggle triggers humbleness which demands appreciation. However if you give someone something that they don't know the value of they will surely waste it. One thing that I have learned is the importance of loving family and leaving them where they are. Your journey will be lonely and those who seem closest to you will smile in your face as they tear you down behind your back.
You're no fool; you know that they're many who are waiting patiently on the downfall of anyone who's gradually growing. You can spot a phony a mile away because they overtly use a brighter smile to compensate their wicked heart. Your question is why waste energy and effort to hate him who has nothing? You must remember that your enemies are like the devil; they hate your potential. The more you work toward your goal the less time you will spend pretending.

Warren J Davis Jr. always said "What you have today is a reflection of what you did yesterday, and what you do today will be a reflection of what you will have tomorrow. Enjoying life means enjoying the many moments, and remembering that every moment is a gift given by GOD. If you respond with a complaint, saying that there were many moments that you didn't care for. I would curiously inquired "how do you complain about a GIFT?" I was once asked if I considered an obstacle a GIFT? I responded by saying "of course NOT, but the lesson learned from a struggle will sustain you and your offspring (who will listen) until the end of time."

Life will teach you that trying to change a person who doesn't want to change will quickly create an enemy. It's interesting how everyone has a PHD when it comes to analyzing someone else's downfalls and struggles. However people become illiterate when it comes to analyzing their own.

My mother told me that no one wants to see their own situation because they will be forced to see themselves, and if they see themselves, they will be forced to blame themselves, and no one wants to blame themselves because they will be forced to grow and no one wants to grow because it takes hard work and dedication. And No one wants to put in the hard work and dedication because it immediately removes them from their comfort zone.

Juan had my full attention, not to discredit the messenger but if you knew MY BROTHER like I do, you would understand that this message was truly from GOD.

Great Gifts were Given, During My Journey To Success 7/26/13@10:05pm

My cousin Kimberly advised me to be careful of whom I share my accomplishments with because everyone who laughs and smiles are not tickled. Charles Whitman (*Famous Actor and friend*) told me that its hell to get on, but when I'm on, I'm on. My mother told me to fear nothing but failure because true failure is giving up. My aunt Gloria Haynes always challenged me when it came to my vocabulary. I remember her saying that "it's power in words therefore you must know what words mean and you must know how to use them."

My sister (Shiquita Davis) told me to get away and see something different, in addition she assured me that years later, those who I left behind will be doing the same thing that they were doing before I left. I admire my sisters strong will to overcome her obstacles in life. My grandmother (Ollie May White) told me to never fool myself and to take heed when something isn't white in the milk. My oldest brother (Warren J. Davis Jr.) taught me that perception is everything however I didn't understand it until I became a marketing major.

Life taught me that 100 no's is what separates me from one yes. While Hill Harper (Author/Actor) and I sat and talked, he told me that the more I owned the more I will control, and the more I control, the more powerful I will become. My dad told me that I only get one turn on this mary-go-round on earth; therefore I should work hard and enjoy the ride. Life has taught me not to focus on a woman before 5:00pm because the opposite sex is a distraction that can cost me a productive day.

Prior relationships have taught me that it's hard (Impossible) to change people but it's harder (even more impossible) to change people that don't want to change. Others mistakes have proven that a moment of passion can lead to a lifetime of pain. My uncle (Dr. Gaylane Carson) always told me that a man without an agenda is going nowhere. My aunt Ophelia Smith (Author of: LIFE ~ You Can Escape!) often reminded me that I would go far in life, never to second guess myself, and whatever I wanted to do, do it, and do it well. My cousin Vanessa Mcalister and I were always full of laughs and love, however she continued to remind me to stay the course.

I remember sitting back stage with Gaston while working on the Ellen Show. I was discouraged therefore I sat quiet in my seat while watching Gaston peak on to the main floor to see the special guest. I wasn't a big sports fan therefore Kobe Bryant didn't impress me. However Gaston kept insisting that I should come stand on the main floor next to him.

He told me that I needed to feel the energy that the room produced from the reaction of these celebrity guests. He was right; the atmosphere was pure, positive, and very addictive. I smiled as Gaston assured me that one-day that would be us. God has the most interesting ways of encouraging you during discouraging times.

- Enjoy the Moment

8/11/2013@12:43am

My grandmother smiled at me while saying "I'm the one who shot the key out of the hole, ram shacked the dead, and put the live on a wonder." Don't feel bad; she had to explain it to me as well. It was her way of saying that she was a bad mother, shut yo mouth. But putting all jokes aside, she's that, and more. My grandmother (Ollie White Burchette) is 92 and the fact that she's owned, modified and sold over 70 properties (houses) is impressive and commendable, but when you consider the fact that she did all this with a 3rd grade education, it's remarkable.

When I ask my grandmother about her pass she always looked away in a daze while slowly shaking her head saying "it was tuff". She told me that it's interesting how no one wants the struggle but everyone wants the final product. My grandmother often says that the more you have, the more others want and the more you give the more others will take. Let her tell it she's poor, and barely making it, and all the money she made has been spent years ago. Ollie white would support her case by saying "money is different now day than it was back then."

I wouldn't dare say that my grandmother is untruthful however I have yet to see a poor person buy a $40,000.00 dollar house in cash, and spend thousands more out of pocket, on modifications. I saw my grandmother two days ago and asked her where she was going, she told me to a car dealership just to eyeball some nice cars that she wish she could afford.

I asked her if she found one on the showroom floor that she really liked how would she pay for it, she smiled and said "cash baby boy" and I began to smile as usual. I learned a lot from my grandmother, she taught me not to show everything I have. The average person will sit in limbo using what they don't have as an excuse that stops them from their destiny. My Grandmother only focused on what she had and her MOTTO was "this will do."

I asked her what's something that she really enjoyed doing. She responded by saying praising the lord. Truth is told, one can easily tell that my grandmother has been kept by a higher power much greater than her.

Sometimes in life God won't give you a textbook, but instead, he'll become your professor and teach you what man can't.

•   Time will tell

OWN (moment) IT

I unconsciously pulled out my phone and listed to my voice mail. To my surprise I sat in disbelief as my mind processed what my ears was hearing. "Hello Don, my name is Talia Robinson Human Resources Director at Oprah Winfrey Network (OWN). I am calling you concerning a position that you applied for in our creative department, if you're still interested please call us back, we hope to meet with you soon." I was overwhelmed with excitement. The first person I called was my oldest brother, he was immediately happy for me but curious to know if I called her back. When I told him no his response was "why are you still on the phone with me."

I called Talia (*HR@OWN*) back but she didn't answer. I suffered to long to play it cool therefore I immediately called her back until she picked up. She knew exactly who it was when she answered the phone. I admitted that I was almost in tears when I heard her voice on my answering machine. She smiled and assured me that she understood how tight the job market is. She asked me if I wanted to meet with the Vice President of the creative department on October 7th,8th or 9th?

I asked if we could have a skype meeting because I didn't have the funds to fly to LA for an interview. She apologized and told me that he didn't do skype interviews. During the moment of silence she asked me where I was momentarily located. I told her that I was in Chicago visiting family while in-between jobs. She smiled and said "Well the VP's office is in Chicago (Harpo Studio) if you want me to set up an appointment for tomorrow morning.

I was sure to do my homework on Kristian Crummie as soon as I got home. I needed to find information about him that would create a common ground, making me rememberable after the interview. My friend Zen called me from Cali and asked me what I was doing. I told her how God worked in my behalf allowing me to have the interview in Chicago.

I continued by telling her that I was researching the requirement and comparing it to my resume so I can justify the reason that I was the one for the position. She responded by saying that one could easily see that God ordained me to have the position. She told me to get some rest because God have already made the way and the interview wont be nowhere near as tuff as I think.

To my surprise she was right, he and I was around the same age. I arrived the next day at Harpo Studio thirty minutes prior to my 9:30am appointment. I allowed my personality to shine.

All of my doubts disappeared when my oldest brother/-mentor sent me a text 20mins earlier that day saying, "you're the smartest person I know." I sat in front of the VP at exactly 9:30am. He was impressed with my conversation; everything that I studied about the company wasn't necessary, because he just wanted to know about who I was as an individual.

Zen was right this interview was easier than a slice of pie. I was carful not to discuss compensation however I continued to reiterate how passionate I was about growth. Twenty minutes passed, he asked if I had anymore question, I said no, we stood, shook hands, and he told me that he would keep in touch. I left feeling good.

Exactly one month later I followed up with HR and to my surprise they hired someone else for the position. I sat and smirked, while thinking to myself "Ms. Winfrey and I will have a lot to talk about while sitting on her couch".

- My hidden drive is the need to be someone who matters

Challenge

I challenge you to understand that I am NOT a GENIUS. I stumble and fumble the ball of opportunity each and every time. I'm insecure, unlearned, and broken. However when connecting to God, he allows himself to speak through me.

Truth is told, it's not mine, but it's God's ingenious thoughts that are immediately exposed therefore I challenge you to keep God 1st. I challenge you to allow God to use you. Understand that God's utilization for you do not always produce a glamorous spotlight. In order to be used by God, you will actually have to be used. Sometimes in order to be used by God you have to be humiliated, kicked and beaten.

In addition understand that God is feeling more pain during the publishing process than you are. Don't be afraid of struggle because it creates experience, and the experiences create substance. Please realize the there won't be any substance without experience. I challenge you to embrace your good ideas, and execute them.

Practice the art of self-discipline because if you don't you will become a slave to that which controls you. I challenge you to motivate, educate and liberate yourself and others. I challenge you to remember that the best investments in life are: your Spiritual connection, health, relationships, real estate, and education. I challenge you to dig deeper, jump higher, run faster, and believe the impossible. I challenge you to stare adversity in the face, knowing that you have already won. Belief is a lifestyle and a stubborn focus that can't be altered. I challenge you to find your purpose, embrace it and make the impact that you were destined to make. Understand that people don't hate you; they hate the fact that they can't be you (you're special).

I need you to be the example, which is a selfless act that is needed to guide others to greatness. I pray that you will love, believe, and apply yourself to the fullest and I understand that this is easier said than done. Please don't use my downfalls as ammunition while gossiping amongst one another. Be wise enough to learn from other people's mistakes and don't use their downfall and an excuse for your stumbling stone. The more you sit under wisdom the quicker you will become wiser.

Take responsibilities for your actions; dust yourself off, and be better than you were yesterday. Please don't make the awful mistake of trying to get something for nothing, because I assure you that this route will cost you triple the heartache. Please understand that nothing is free and I assure you that you'll pay one way or another. Think before you act, walk before you run, and learn before you lead. As I stated earlier love self, believe in self, be proactive, be accountable for your actions, and allow the creator to work in your behalf.

Remember that your actions make them doubt you. However the fruits of your faith will make them question everything they learned in school (*Sens Musiq/international artist*) Stay encouraged and despite your limitation you must continue to dream.

I challenge you to allow God to be your hero, saving yourself from self. Honestly ask yourself these questions: "What do I want, Why do I want it, how bad do I want it, and what am I willing to sacrifice to get it?" No matter how hard thing appear I challenge you to hold on because your life depends on it. **During your daily decisions I challenge you to choose logic over emotion, assets over liability, and profits over wages**. Last but not least there are 86,400 seconds in a day and 168 hours in a week, monitor your time, and use it wisely.

The closer I get to the end the more I begin to think about the beginning. My words rang loud as I reflect on my FORWARD. "Please don't do as I do; because I'm far from perfect. But instead follow the spiritually inspired stroke of the pen that paints the portrait like a brush, which will carefully guide you on the journey toward your success. I question if I am qualified to write a self-help book. How can I tell you how to overcome your obstacles when I'm standing stagnate trying to over come mine?

The sheriff knocked on my door at 6am, issuing me a letter of foreclosure. I walked back to my room and sat on the edge of my bed in silence, as my mind immediately raced to find a solution. Usually people wait until they've reached their pinnacle of success before writing a self-help book. However I promise you, that well before this book finds you, I will be okay.

It's interesting how people gravitate to those who are financially stable but mentally unbalanced. I apologize that I don't have a flashy Lamborghini nor a Maserati to capture your attention; but if interested, I'm willing to give you my scattered thoughts. I encourage you to never discredit the power of a man's thoughts, because in all actuality it was someone's thought that created the Lamborghini and the Maserati.

Please allow me to give you what pain gave me, in hopes that you will learn from the lesson, without experiencing the dreadful sting."

Irrefutable

by
Donamechi ~~Donamechi~~
X.
Davis

Follow Mr. Davis's Blog at

scatteredthoughts15.tumblr.com